Celebrate each season!

Bruce Sibold

The Seasons on Eighty Acres
Copyright © 2018 Bruce Siebold
Published by Rusk Prairie Consulting Group
Design by Lindsay Lindner

www.eightyacresphotography.com
bruce@eightyacresphotography.com

All rights reserved. No part of this publication may be reproduced in whole or in part, or stored on a retrieval system, or transmitted in any form or by any means, electronic, mechanical, photocopying, recording or otherwise without written permission from the publisher.

ISBN: 978-0-9979097-1-5

Acknowledgments

The following individuals have all played key roles in making this book a reality. I want to thank...

My family
Who have been constant cheerleaders. For their faith, love and encouragement.

My mentors Bill Buell and Chris Smith
Who are always there to teach, encourage, support and listen.

My graphic designer, Lindsay Lindner
Who with her creative talents somehow managed to organize my photographic chaos into a beautifully designed book.

My editors extraordinaire, Richard Timmerman, Joy Bergstrand and Allison Siebold-Guzman
Who with patience and understanding provided razor-sharp insight and tough love.

My best friend and wife, Terry Siebold
Who has been my constant supporter throughout each season of my life. This book is dedicated to you.

Introduction

For the past twenty-seven years (nearly ten thousand days), I have lived on a parcel of land known as 'Eighty Acres' located near Menomonie, Wisconsin. Eighty Acres is a beautiful piece of land. More than sixty acres are rolling woodlands with a variety of trees, including oak, maple, cherry, birch, aspen, poplar and pine. Nestled below the hills are twenty acres of grassland and almost directly in the center of the property is my family's home, built in 1991.

Over these many years, and during my daily walks on the land, Eighty Acres became my photography studio. I have been accused by some that my daily walks are simply a ploy to avoid my chores. I will admit, depending upon my "to do" list, there may be some truth to this claim. But I believe there is a much more important reason to take these treks. For deep within, an inner voice calls to me. Urging me to become one with the earth and to capture her many moods, voices and stories with my camera.

"Seasons" is my second book and a photographic journey through each season on Eighty Acres. This book presents a compendium of my favorite nature photos for each season of the year. I urge you to read the book slowly. See each photo and read each story through the eyes of a child. Recall the first time you saw a whitetail fawn, an arching rainbow or the mysterious frost on your window. This book is intended to give you permission to bring you back to an earlier day and relive the beauty and awe of the land we live upon. In the end, I hope this book will help you...

SEE the beauty in each and every day.
FEEL in your soul a special calmness and harmony the Earth Mother brings to us.
BELIEVE there are mysteries and secrets that we cannot explain or understand.
PROTECT this land for our children and grandchildren.
BE MINDFUL of the Earth Mother's gifts with each step you take, each color you see, each fragrance you inhale, each melody you hear, each flavor you taste and each moment you live.
Enjoy each day and each season's journey.

Bruce Siebold 2018

Seasons
on Eighty Acres

Eighty Acres
PHOTOGRAPHY

Profile

Growing up on a dairy farm in northwest Wisconsin provided me the freedom to connect with the land. In 1991, my wife Terry and I built our home on an eighty-acre parcel of land located near Menomonie, Wisconsin. Immediately the land became my photographic studio, and ever since, the subject of thousand of photographs. My photo collection includes a variety of nature themes including landscapes, sunsets, wildlife, flowers and birds.

Throughout the years, I have worked hard to train my eyes to see the nuances of the land. So, each day I pack my camera bag, and with hope, set off to discover and attempt to capture the land's spirit with my camera lens.

Eighty Acres. Always inspiring. Always challenging. Always providing hope for the perfect shot just around the corner.

Photo credit: Allison Siebold-Guzman

SPRING

Spring is my favorite season.
A new beginning with each sunrise.
Hopeful.
Fearless.
Too young to understand.
Too young to know better.
Running fast with my eyes closed.
The season I knew there would be someone to love.
Someone I just had not yet met.

Bluebirds Return to Eighty Acres

Each year near the 1st of April the Eastern Bluebirds return to Eighty Acres. Ten bluebird boxes await their arrival and when they do arrive immediately the bird battles begin. Bluebirds, wrens, sparrows and swallows all vie for the same property. There are no guarantees who will win the wars, but enough bluebirds succeed each year to make their home on Eighty Acres. An ample food supply awaits the bluebirds. Elderberries and a wide variety of insects keep them well fed throughout their summer stay. Their nests will have two to seven pale blue eggs in one to three broods each summer. The bluebirds are a sure sign of spring. Welcome back to Eighty Acres!

Uff Da!

Mid-April and over a foot of new snow blanketed Eighty Acres. Enough! My 98-year-old Swedish mother has a word for this type of bafflement, dismay, or surprise. Uff Da! Mom, the deer and I would all agree.

Birth on Eighty Acres

With tottering legs, the fawns arrive on Eighty Acres in early May. Beautifully camouflaged and weighing only six to eight pounds at birth, they soon learn that their long legs can be used for escaping predators or just jumping for sheer joy. While looking for trillium I was fortunate to spot this fawn. Instinct told the fawn to freeze hoping I would pass by. After several photos, I slowly and quietly backed away knowing the fawn would soon be reunited with its mother. Welcome to Eighty Acres little one.

Welcome Home

After six months away, the robins return to Eighty Acres. An undeniable sign of spring. Welcome home robin!

Turkey Nesting Time

I was fortunate to discover a turkey nest on Eighty Acres. The nest was a shallow depression and the eggs perfectly blended into the oak leaves. Turkey hens will lay one egg per day and the eggs require an incubation period of 26 days. Not long after this photo was taken, I was disappointed to find the eggs broken and scattered about. The nest must have been discovered by hungry raccoons, crows or fox. The circle of life continues on Eighty Acres.

Out Foxing the Fox on Eighty Acres

During my time on Eighty Acres, I have seen only a fleeting glimpse of a red fox. While overlooking the valley from my house windows, I saw this red fox moving slowly and cautiously across the field. Grabbing my camera I raced out and quietly tiptoed to the ridge of the hill. Fortunately the wind was blowing in the perfect direction so that the fox was unaware that I stood only forty yards away on the hill above him. With no time to check my camera settings I quickly clicked my first shot. Not good! Out of focus and an unnecessary flash sent light across the valley.

When the fox turned his head away from me, I adjusted the camera settings and prayed I hadn't blown the opportunity. Slowly the fox began to move parallel to me and then for some unknown reason turned and slowly walked directly at me! Thirty yards. Twenty yards. Ten yards. My camera was now clicking five pictures a second. Still he came directly at me. Twenty feet. Ten feet. As I tried to hold the camera steady, the fox bolted to my right and quickly disappeared behind a pine tree. Wow! Over in a matter of seconds. I finally got the shot I had been seeking. It's the day I outfoxed the fox. Or maybe the day I just got lucky on Eighty Acres.

On My Belly on Eighty Acres

Taking time to slow down and look at the little things can be rewarding. Such was the case with the Bracken Ferns on Eighty Acres... They are beautiful ferns, often growing upwards to three feet tall and giving a soft tropical look to the floor of the woods. For many years I simply walked by the emerging feathery fronds. Then one day I slowed down, got down on my belly, and noticed how the fronds unfurl in such unique shapes. Early in spring their shapes are often referred to as "fiddle heads". But this day their shape took on more of an elephant trunk or sea horse appearance The next day I hurried back, once again got on my belly, but discovered that the elephants and sea horses had silently disappeared during the night.

A Buck in Velvet

Each April bucks begin growing their new antlers. As the antlers develop, they are covered in soft, hairy skin known as velvet. The velvet is filled with blood vessels and nerves. In the fall when the antlers are fully formed, the velvet is no longer nourished and falls off. What remains is true antler bone.

Bear Scrape

During bear mating season (May and June), black bear will often visit Eighty Acres. To mark their territory they will claw, bite and rub trees and posts. I have seen black bear several times on Eighty Acres, but never with my camera in hand! Capturing a photo of a black bear is on my "to do" list.

Destruction

During the night my bird feeders were destroyed; evidence that a hungry and determined black bear feasted on sunflower seeds, suet and nyjer seed.

Close Enough!

The hungry skunk appeared under my bird feeder munching on sunflower seeds and bits of suet. A photo opportunity? I cautiously approached the skunk, but it was so intent on eating that it would not look at me. What to do? Why not get its attention by tossing a snowball. Bad throw. Missed! My next snowball hit the skunk's nose. Up came its head. Up came my camera. Click. I quickly backed away. Not my best photo. But, close enough!

Creamy or Chunky?

I've attempted to photograph blue jays numerous times, but more often than not I have failed. Blue jays love to grab their food and quickly fly away. In an attempt to slow them down, I placed globs of peanut butter on a branch and then placed peanuts in each sticky spot. This blue jay grabbed the peanut, gave me a suspicious look, and quickly flew away to enjoy his sticky treat. This experiment got me thinking. I wonder… do blue jays prefer creamy or chunky peanut butter?

His Last Bed

Perhaps he struggled to find a safe place to lay down, rest, close his eyes and fall asleep. I discovered his bones scattered about in the spring and honored him with a prayer to the Earth Mother. Thank you for his strength, his beauty and for choosing to make his last bed on Eighty Acres.

Sweet Tooth

During spring the flame orange and black Baltimore Orioles return to Eighty Acres from their winter home in Central America. The orioles arrive with big, bold and melodious songs. They quickly begin to build hanging pouch-like nests and will lay four to seven blueish-gray eggs. Orioles feast on insects, caterpillars and moths. But their favorite food will be grape jam and they really don't care if you offer the generic brand!

Trouble!

Groundhogs have many names including ground pig, whistler and red monk. On Eighty Acres I also give them many different names... some not repeatable! Groundhogs are great diggers and with their powerful legs and thick claws seem to enjoy digging in my flower beds and under my garden shed. I'm all for coexisting on Eighty Acres, but strongly encourage all groundhogs to respect my space! The photo above shows a groundhog standing on its hind legs with his mouth full of oak leaves intent on building a nest under my terrace steps. Please! Go away or there will be big TROUBLE!

Coyote Den

Nestled beneath an old tree stump, I discovered a coyote den. With camera in hand and more than a bit of fear, I quietly approached the den and captured this photo of a coyote pup. Look carefully and you will see the ears of a second pup in the lower left of the den. Hoping for more photos, I returned the next day only to find the den abandoned. Mom must have been watching and relocated to a safer and quieter place.

Good Fortune

It is an exciting day when a bald eagle visits Eighty Acres. Native Americans believe eagles represent wisdom, strength, spirituality and good fortune. Note the beautiful pale yellow eye. Eagles possess amazing eyesight which is four to eight times stronger than the human eye. With a wing span of more than eight feet, they are able to dive at speeds of greater than 75 miles per hour. An amazing and majestic bird. Yes…good fortune came to Eighty Acres.

Eye To Eye

The Ruffed Grouse makes its home on Eighty Acres and is often heard beating its wings in a rhythmic drum-like sound. If threatened, it will rely on its perfect camouflage and hope the danger will pass. While walking Eighty Acres trail this Ruffed Grouse and I surprised each other. We both remained perfectly still and looked into each other's eyes for several minutes. Ever so slowly I raised my camera and snapped this photo. We then continued our walks in separate directions.

Jack-in-the-Pulpit Discovered

I discovered the berries of this Jack-In-The-Pulpit flower under a patch of thick blackberry vines. The name of this unusual flower comes from its hood shaped leaves that protects the club shaped appendage. With a little imagination it looks like a preacher standing in an old fashioned pulpit. In the fall, its berries are bright green but as they ripen become deep red. The birds soon discovered these berries and, in just a short time, they were gone. Beautiful discovery!

It's the Truth

Do you remember the 1946 Disney song "Zip-A-Dee-Doo-Dah?" The song reminds us to celebrate each day because there is "plenty of sunshine heading my way" and "Mr. Bluebird's on my shoulder". The bluebirds are back to Eighty Acres and yes… "It's the truth. It's actual. Everything is satisfactual."

SUMMER

Summer is my favorite season.
With open windows I invite the night in to sleep with me.
Distant thunder.
Sweet smelling earth.
A train whistle spreads slowly across the prairie.
Confident.
Certain.
I boldly welcome each morning sun.
The season I knew I first loved you.

Mindful of the Beauty

Early each summer I discover bleeding heart flowers blooming on Eighty Acres. The heart-shaped, fuchsia colored petals make me pause and enjoy the flower's bold color and unique shape. I will let the poets speak to the symbolism and romantic connotations of the flower. For me it is a simple reminder to slow down and be mindful of the beauty in each day.

From South America to Eighty Acres

It's a long trip from northern South America, but this Scarlet Tanager finally arrived back to Eighty Acres. The bird is stunning with a blood red body and deep black wings. Lucky for me, it stopped by the feeder for a quick snack and drink of water. Then it was gone. I seldom see tanagers in the summer because they spend most of their time high in the forest canopy. Their main concern throughout the season is the Brown-headed Cowbird. The crafty cowbird raids the Scarlet Tanager's nest, removes the eggs and replaces them with their own. Unable to tell the difference between the eggs, the tanager hatches and feeds the baby cowbirds until they leave the nest. Welcome back Scarlet Tanager and watch out for the cowbirds!

Metamorphosis on Eighty Acres

Each year Eighty Acres experiences the magic and mystery of the Monarch Butterfly's transformation from a tiny egg to a dancing butterfly. The caterpillar (or larva stage) is a true eating machine. It eats milkweed leaves for several days before spinning into a pupa. Within two weeks the adult monarch wiggles free and after two hours of figuring out what wings are for, begins its search for sweet nectar. Due to a decreasing supply of milkweed, the monarch population has declined in recent years. On Eighty Acres I now mow around the milkweed and even plant milkweed in my flower gardens. Plant milkweed seed in your backyard and you too can enjoy the beautiful magic of the Earth Mother.

Shared With Me Today

Monarch butterflies often visit Eighty Acres. Dressed in black and orange with white spots, this monarch spoke to me in a language I understood but am often afraid to acknowledge. Birth, change and making way for a new generation are part of life's journey. Just as the monarch, I hope that each day of my life can be filled with the same joy, excitement, courage, and beauty the monarch shared with me.

Beautiful and Smart

Birds like the Indigo Bunting generally put me in a wild dash for my camera and a prayer that I am able to capture its beauty before it wings away. Seldom seen on Eighty Acres, it will occasionally be spotted at the bird bath. They nest in dense shrubs, often along roadsides with their nests one to three feet above ground. They leave Eighty Acres each fall and head to the tropics for the winter. Not only beautiful, but smart!

Thank You Sun

After several days of clouds and rain on Eighty Acres, today I felt the sun warm my face. As the sun slowly set behind the horizon, I felt at peace and knew I had been blessed.

Calling for Wiley E. Coyote

Our world is filled with stories about cute bunny rabbits. Brer Rabbit, Disney's Thumper, Bigwig from the classic novel Watership Down, the White Rabbit in Alice in Wonderland, Looney Tunes Bugs Bunny and the always adorable Easter Bunny. You will find an abundance of rabbits on Eighty Acres and they all have one thing in common. They enjoy eating my flowers, shrubs and trees! Their cuteness is fading fast. Where is Wiley E. Coyote when I need him?

Brave in Heart

Eighty Acres is home to four types of squirrels; gray, fox, black and red. The smallest of the squirrels is the red squirrel, which I believe is the most fierce and courageous. It measures only twelve inches from head to tail but will defend its territory like no other. Without fear, I have seen them attack much larger squirrels, chipmunks, rabbits and even crows. Fiercely territorial, they even stare me down or chatter their disapproval if I attempt to venture into their space. Small in stature, but truly brave in heart.

This is My Day

Each day lily blossoms for only twenty-four hours, and then it is gone. But the flower does not regret its fleeting time. Rather than be filled with remorse, the lily uses its short time to celebrate, sing, dance, and to enjoy the moment. Each day comes but once. Thank you for this lesson Earth Mother. Today I will enjoy each moment and be grateful, joyful, kind and generous. This is my day!

An SOS for Help?

Eighty Acres is now home to a pair of red-headed woodpeckers. Once common across southern Canada and east-central United States, the loss of its nesting habitat has resulted in severe population decline, and moved the woodpeckers into a threatened status. As I walk Eighty Acres, I hear them singing their songs and drumming on dead elm trees. Perhaps they are sending me an SOS for help?

A Softer and Gentler Type of Fireworks

The nation celebrates Independence Day with fireworks that shake and rattle the skies. The Earth Mother also celebrates each day with her own spectacular fireworks. Just as beautiful… a softer and gentler type of fireworks.

Quietly Shares a Secret

Dancing and whirling she announces her arrival dressed in a gown of silky dark gossamer trimmed with red, orange and yellow buttons. She sips the coneflower's sweet nectar, flutters her delicate translucent wings and quietly shares a secret with me.

Pileated Woodpecker on Eighty Acres!

When I see the shy Pileated Woodpecker on Eighty Acres I often have flashbacks to the 1950s Saturday morning cartoon shows of Bugs Bunny, Daffy Duck and Woody Woodpecker. The Pileated Woodpecker is one of the largest woodpeckers in North America with a wing-span of nearly 30 inches. It makes its home on Eighty Acres due to the large number of dead Elm trees. The Pileated Woodpecker is a real "head banger" and seems never to worry about headaches or following concussion protocol. With its strong beak, it hammers the trees, chipping out long rectangular holes to feed on insects, ants and beetle larvae found within the dead trees.

Pileated Woodpeckers mate in April and make their nest in a hollowed out tree about 10-15 feet above the ground. The female lays three or more eggs and both the male and female stay together as they raise their young.

The call of the Pileated Woodpecker is very distinctive and somewhat eerie. Many people refer to it as a "jungle bird" sound. Listen carefully... on some quiet evening you may hear her calling. Then you will know you have a Pileated Woodpecker in your backyard, or that it's simply Woody Woodpecker returning from your childhood memories to remind you of those wonderful Saturday morning cartoons.

Sunsets on Eighty Acres

I have now lived on Eighty Acres for nearly 10,000 days and during that time have captured hundreds of the Earth Mother's sunsets. Taken in 2014, this is one of my all time favorites. Over the years, it has become a ritual to say a thank you sun prayer at the end of each day. It is a prayer softly sent to the Earth Mother thanking her for all she has given me that day. Sunsets are free. I encourage you to take time to raise your eyes and receive these beautiful gifts.

Life Journeys Cross

◀ A twelve-spotted skimmer dragonfly visited Eighty Acres. It danced in the wind and its transparent wings reflected the early morning sunlight. For a brief second the dragonfly gently sat upon my hand, and in that moment our lives crossed.

Fast Mover

Every summer Ruby-throated Hummingbirds migrate to Eighty Acres from Central America. They weigh three to four grams, (less than the weight of a nickel) and generally fly 25-40 mph. Two amazing facts about hummingbirds are that their wings beat between 60-80 times PER SECOND and they are the only bird that can fly backwards! Once the hummingbirds arrive on Eighty Acres they seem to be in perpetual motion visiting each flower and the hummingbird feeder several times each day. One gear. One speed. One beautiful and amazing fast mover! ▶

Swallowed by the Fog

On an early morning the Earth Mother was dressed in gray as a heavy wet fog hung over Eighty Acres. While sitting quietly in my photo blind, a hawk silently glided in and landed atop the dead rabbit. After a second or two, it lifted skyward. I heard its wings beating against the heavy air as it rose in the gray sky. I quickly clicked this photo just before the hawk was swallowed by the fog.

King Tut Sunset

The silhouette of the King Tut plants waves goodbye to the setting sun. Time to quietly reflect upon the day's many blessings.

One Thousand Trees

It has been said that when you plant a tree, you are giving a gift to the next generation. Over the past 27 years, more than 1,000 pine trees have been planted on Eighty Acres. I hope the trees will be appreciated by the next generation. But in the mean time, each tree helps me frame an Eighty Acres sunset.

Woven World

While walking on Eighty Acres, I abruptly stopped with my face coming within a few inches of this spider's web. As the sun touched the morning dew, it gave me a glimpse into the beautiful woven home of the spider. Blue lights hung on each street corner throughout his city, with fireworks in the town center. The spider was busy designing new pathways and was ever alert for possible visitors or intruders. As the sun moved, the spider's world slowly disappeared. I stepped aside and walked on, hoping to visit the magical woven world once again tomorrow.

Eighty Acres Fireworks!

Happy 4th of July! I found this tall grass growing along the edge of my pine trees. As the setting sunlight reflected off its tassels, it reminded me of fireworks. No thunderous explosions, no ooohs, no aaahs. Just a quiet, calm and reflective moment that reminded me of the many moods and unending beauty on Eighty Acres.

The Earth Mother Sighed

The powerful diesel tractor swept through the alfalfa and clover hay field rumbling the ground all around the mother turkey and her egg filled nest. The mother turkey had kept her eggs warm and protected from harm for over three weeks, but now her world shook with an unfamiliar sound and vibration. Not wanting to abandon the nest, she and the eggs were swept up into the haybine's razor sharp blades and rollers. The crows were the first to discover the shattered nest. Soon turkey vultures and a bald eagle claimed their share of the feast. And then... the Earth Mother sighed.

Tigers in the Sky

During the summer months Eastern Tiger Swallowtails often dance gently on the tree tops of Eighty Acres. They are the largest butterflies on Eighty Acres with a wing span between three to six inches. From the tree tops they flutter to earth and gather the sweet nectar from coneflowers, bee balm and bull thistles. From May to September they swirl about the land, lay their eggs and, in keeping with the Earth Mother's plan, the eggs soon become the next generation of tigers in the sky.

Thanked Me With a Song

The sparrow slipped into the cool bird bath water and washed its dusty wings. It twisted, shook and danced, sending hundreds of water droplets flying into the afternoon sunshine. Cooled and cleaned, it thanked me for the cool water with a song and then quickly flew away.

We Are All Connected

For several days smoke from numerous western forest fires brought blood red sunsets to Eighty Acres. This makes me mindful of the fragile interconnected planet we are all living upon. Beautiful sunsets on Eighty Acres... charred earth, smoke and pain thousands of miles away. One earth, one circle, one humanity, one opportunity to protect her for our children and grandchildren.

Living Life as a Sunflower

Each day the sunflower stands tall and bold and chooses to turn its head to the sunlight. The sunflower does not seek the darkness nor the demons of the day. Rather it chooses hope and sunshine, savoring the delicious moments of each day. A simple lesson... but at times so difficult to remember.

With a Gentle Kiss

The Painted Lady Butterfly flirted with each flower in the garden as it danced, caressed, fluttered, spread its wings, and then suddenly said goodbye with a gentle kiss.

I Ran Like a Coward!

Coexisting with paper wasps on Eighty Acres requires one to be alert at all times. Paper wasps build their nests by gathering fiber from dead wood and mixing it with saliva to construct their paper-like homes. Once built, the queen lays one egg in each hexagonal cell and in a few weeks the new wasps hatch. I was lucky enough to capture this photo as they emerged from their cells. With several wasps buzzing around my head and knowing the pain of a sting… I ran like hell. Like a coward!

Bad Hair Day

◀ Can't a bluebird have a bad hair day along with a little attitude? I just had my bath and I'm air drying my feathers. So go away! I'll look much prettier tomorrow.

My Favorite Flower

Each year dozens of dahlias are planted and grown on Eighty Acres. They are my favorite flower and come in dozens of varieties with blossoms ranging in size from two to twelve inches. The history of dahlias goes back to the Aztecs where the tubers were used both as a food source and for medical treatments. Today the beautiful flower is a rich source of nectar for the butterflies, bees and birds on Eighty Acres. ▶

1 in 10,000

It is rare to see a black squirrel on Eighty Acres. They are not a separate variety or species; rather they are eastern gray squirrels with a genetic condition called melanism. It is estimated that this genetic condition occurs approximately once out of every ten thousand births.

Throw Away the Key

Each night the raccoon slinks, steals, lurks, swipes, creeps, pilfers and sneaks around Eighty Acres. I now know why raccoons wear bandit masks. Lock up the burglar. Throw away the key!

Black Eyed Susans

◀ As I near the flower terrace, hundreds of black eyes follow me. Watching me closely. Suspicious. Hoping a scissors is not in my hand.

Only Memories Remain

Once an Eighty Acres landmark, the Aero Motor Windmill with its bullet-riddled wind vane, stood tall atop a hill for decades. Covered with grapevines, it toppled during a severe summer windstorm. Now only this photo and my memories of it remain. ▶

Eighty Acres Rainbow

After an early evening thunderstorm, the rainbow spread its arc over Eighty Acres. A joyous gift for today and a promise for tomorrow.

FALL

Fall is my favorite season.
A primal voice speaks to me,
To make all things ready.
To harvest the garden.
Stack the firewood.
Bake apple pies.
Store the hoe and hose.
Pick the last dahlia bouquet.
Thank the setting sun.
The season I knew I would grow old only with you.

Morning Prayer

Early morning stillness. Coffee cup in hand. I watch the sun chase the dark away. The sunrise is dressed in bold colors. Reds, pinks, oranges, blacks and grays. I softly whisper my morning prayer and hope I will celebrate this day through joy, forgiveness, and in some way, make the world a better place. Amen.

The Scars Remain

Earlier this fall the Earth Mother sent howling 50+ mph winds to Eighty Acres. Like a heavyweight boxer the wind punched and jabbed the house all night long, rattling the windows and causing the chimes to sing eerie songs. The following day I found the walking trails littered with branches, two uprooted trees and paper birch bark ripped, torn and laid back against the tree trunks. The siege is over. The scars remain.

The Elm's Last Sunset

This giant elm tree stood tall and strong for decades on Eighty Acres. To the cattle below it gave shade. To the birds, it provided a place to nest, and for me, it framed a thousand sunsets. But now it is dead. Soon it will be cut down and the wood used to keep me warm this winter. In the days ahead, I plan to walk by and rest upon its stump and remember the elm's outstretched arms, its grace in the wind, and its last sunset.

Blood Moon Over Eighty Acres

A blood moon is often associated with doomsday prophecies. But on October 8, 2014, I approached the event with positive anticipation and a great deal of preparation. Eighty Acres provided a front row seat to this rare event where the earth's shadow slowly dims the moon resulting in a global sunset on the moon. The evening arrived and my camera equipment was checked and rechecked for the 10:00 p.m. show time. For an hour and 12 minutes my camera shutter clicked. As the eclipse faded without the world ending, I felt lucky to have captured this wonderful blood moon sitting over Eighty Acres.

What They Didn't Teach Me in School

My teachers did a great job of explaining sunsets as they are related to wavelengths and how sunlight strikes molecules. But not one mentioned how a sunset can speak to your spirit, allow you to dream, imagine a world of peace, provide an appreciation for each breath you take and to allow one to see the wonders of life.

Under the Dead Elm's Bark

A recently fallen elm tree on Eighty Acres revealed the beautiful patterns of tunneling bark beetles. The narrow center cavity is where the adult beetle laid her eggs. As the larvae grew, the egg gallery tunnels increased in diameter. In one month's time, the larvae emerged as a one-eighth inch long, dark reddish brown beetle. The giant elm has died, but if I look carefully, I can still see her beauty under the dry dead bark.

Red-tailed Hawk Visit

On a cool and rainy afternoon, this red-tailed hawk landed in a birch tree located just outside my window. We entered into a staring contest which I quickly lost. As we sat and watched each other, I wondered how long this encounter would last or if our paths would ever cross again. Then suddenly, without warning, it swooped down and glided across the hay field, quickly swallowed up in the tree line. Thanks for stopping by.

An Eighty Acres' Secret

Two decades ago I discovered a roll of rusting barbed wire on Eighty Acres. Although frequently captured with my camera, no photo displayed its beauty, power and purpose as does the solitary rusting barb shown above. What stories does this wire hold? Who was the person who rolled the wire? Did the sharp barbs cut through cloth gloves causing fingers to bleed? Did the person curse? Did the sharp barbs keep the cattle in place? I'll never know. Just one more piece of history lost. One more secret on Eighty Acres.

Last Dahlia

Frost crept over the garden terrace one fall morning, and the dahlias went to sleep. The once vibrant greens, reds, pinks and yellows turned brown and the dahlias slowly lowered their heads upon their hollow stems. Absolutely beautiful dahlias this year. My memories of the dahlias will keep me warm during the winter, and give me hope for the coming spring.

Spirit Tree

Near the very center of Eighty Acres stands an old giant maple tree. Her outstretched arms completely dominate the surrounding area. I have walked past the old maple for many years, but one day she softly whispered to me and asked me to slow down. To linger. To listen to the silence. To see and feel all the things I once missed. Since that time the old maple has become my spirit tree. Nearby is a tree stump where you will often find me sitting and listening as she shares with me her stories, songs and secrets about Eighty Acres.

Shelf Fungi... Not My Cup of Tea

Numerous shelf fungi protrude from this birch tree on Eighty Acres. Shelf fungi attacked the interior hardwood of the tree, causing the core to rot and die. Upon examination, I found them to be very hard and woody with fifteen years of growth rings. Artists have used shelf fungi to create fine etchings or jewelry and some say it can be ground into a powder and used in tea. But I'll pass. It's not my cup of tea.

Maple Leaves on Water

Maple leaves float on a small pool of water on Eighty Acres. During this time of year, many birds and animals visit the pool to sip the cool water. I also visit the pool and let my eyes drink the rich fall colors.

White and Gold

Eighty Acres is in its Fall glory with the white birch framing the golden maple leaves. The Earth Mother is dressed in her coat of many colors… soon to fall asleep under a soft white blanket of snow.

Sumacs' Glory Days

Most days, sumac is simply ignored on Eighty Acres, but each fall its leaves turn a brilliant crimson color and shout for attention. Sumac comes from an ancient word meaning "red" and over the years has been used for a variety of purposes: a tart lemon-like spice, medicinal uses, Indian lemonade, fabric dying and pipe making. On Eighty Acres the sumacs' brilliant color heralds the beginning of the fall season. It's sumacs' time to be on stage, to shine, to shout "look at me." It's sumacs' glory days!

Blowing in the Wind

In the fall milkweed seed pods burst open. The silky parachutes are swept away in the breeze and land gently land throughout Eighty Acres. All summer I watch as the milkweed plants host numerous bees, wasps, butterflies and insects who feast on this important food source. But now the milkweed plants are old, their journey complete. But the Earth Mother is wise, and the next generation of milkweed is already blowing in the wind.

"Wood Day" on Eighty Acres

Each October family and friends gather on Eighty Acres for "wood day." It is an annual event when six to seven full cords of winter firewood are split, hauled and stacked. In between the chopping, hauling and stacking is Badger football to watch, great food, stories and memories to share, laughter, beverages to drink; all under a beautiful canopy of fall colors. Below are "wood day" crews taking a break from their hard work.

A Gift

For six months this maple leaf lived atop Eighty Acres. It danced in the breeze, trembled during thunder storms, provided shelter for the robins and time after time watched me walk by with my camera in tow. While I was sleeping, the maple leaf released its grip and silently swirled down from its lofty perch to land upon my stacked birch firewood. Thank you for this gift.

A Season Remembered

Fall is a time when the Earth Mother paints Eighty Acres with the red, orange and yellow colors from her crayon box. But her mood has changed and her voice has become softer and more reflective, and she now dresses the earth in gentle tan and brown colors. Winter will soon be upon Eighty Acres, but I will not forget the beauty of the fall season.

WINTER

Winter is my favorite season.
Near the fire I huddle.
The icy winds speak to me.
Echoes. Scars.
Forgotten triumphs.
Forgotten disappointments.
Pondering words spoken.
Those unspoken.
Wiser. Knowing all must die to be reborn.
I bow to time.
The season I am warmed by the touch of your hand as we drift off to sleep.

Warm Front Moving In

This beautiful sunset and cloud formation came to rest for a few moments on Eighty Acres' western horizon. Altocumulus clouds generally signal a warm front is approaching. I'm grateful for the soft warm breeze in November and this beautiful sunset.

Snowstorm Blankets Eighty Acres

Early winter and nine inches of heavy wet snow covered both the land and animals. These one-year-old twin whitetail deer seemed both surprised and confused as just the day before they enjoyed green grass and acorns. Patience and hope to all of my Eighty Acres friends. There is much more winter ahead.

The Earth Mother's Icy Necklace

Freezing rain on Eighty Acres sculpted a beautiful icy necklace on the backyard clothesline. The necklace was crafted with the finest colors of sapphire, garnet, emerald, amethyst and amber. Being somewhat fickle, the Earth Mother wore her necklace for only one day and then the warm sunshine came and quietly dropped the icy colors on the snow below.

He Made It!

The hunting season ended and this buck with the broken antler survived the hunters' bullets and arrows. Now his survival will depend upon being ever alert for predators such as coyotes and wolves, as well as outlasting the long, cold, harsh winter ahead.

Red and White

A late November wet snow fell during the early morning hours, covering the landscape in a heavy white soggy blanket. The last red crab apples of the summer season provided a vivid color contrast to the fresh white snow. With the temperature rising, I had just a short time to capture this shot before a soft warm breeze magically melted the snow from the trees.

Sunset and Sunrise

As the Eighty Acres' sunset slips away and the first star appears in the sky, I give thanks for the day and smile knowing that just over the hill, someone is seeing a sunrise.

Earth Mother's Winter Palette

Winter on Eighty Acres and the Earth Mother carefully blends the colors from her palette. She paints the pine's long and silky needles green, with a touch of soft yellow. For the cones she selects ambers, browns, blacks and then trims them with warm tans. She sprinkles the entire tree with snow in various shades of white. Soft, sleepy and subtle.

A Winter Gift

With deep snow and bitter temperatures, wildlife are working hard to find their next meal. Thanks to an ample supply of black sunflower seeds, several northern cardinals have decided to tough it out and spend the winter with me on Eighty Acres. The cardinal, who is a ground feeder, frequents the feeders in the early mornings and again at dusk. Its crimson red body and black hooded mask make for spectacular arrivals and exits, and I never tire of their visits. Thanks for spending the winter with me.

Winter Survival

The hunters set aside their guns and now the deer face a new challenge of surviving the harsh winter ahead. Hopefully their fat reserves and dense winter coats will help them through the deep snow, frigid winds and a depleted food supply. The deer will seek shelter in dense evergreens or the sides of hills that protect them from the wind and offer warming sunshine. They will dig for acorns and browse on oak leaves and small twigs. During most of the day, they will bed down in order to save their limited energy and strength. The Earth Mother has equipped them well. Now all I can do is watch and hope for an early spring and their winter survival.

Foxtail Colors

Frost and early morning sunshine turned this ordinary looking foxtail into a kaleidoscope of colors.

Mindfulness

For several weeks I stepped over these river stones wrapped in ice. Then came the day I finally saw the beauty in the frozen coral-like ice and colorful rock gems. Why did it take me so long to see this beauty? Each day there are countless opportunities to capture the beauty and spirit of the land. Will I be mindful enough to see the beauty today?

Beauty in Her Tears

As the sun melted the snow, the Earth Mother's tears slowly slid downward and froze into a shimmering icy stalactite. Sometimes there can be beauty in a Mother's tears.

Wabi-Sabi

Before the ring necked pheasant died, it crawled under a brush pile on Eighty Acres. The bird's colors were a majestic collage of bright golds, fiery reds, iridescent greens and blues with a bright white collar around its neck. How he died I do not know, but I am thankful for the opportunity to capture the beauty and spirit of this regal bird. As I photographed the bird, I was reminded of a Japanese view of life called Wabi-Sabi, which finds beauty in nature and accepts the natural cycle of birth, growth, aging and death.

Coneflowers in Winter

It is winter on Eighty Acres and the once bright pink, purple and red coneflowers have gone to seed. Frequently visited by bees, butterflies and finches in the summer; the skeleton-like flowers now provide a sharp contrast to the winter snow. The coneflower seeds are now sleeping and will awaken once the soil is warmed by gentle rains and sunshine.

Dressed in White

◀ While I slept, the Earth Mother quietly slipped into a beautiful white gown, a handsome hat and a lovely pair of glittered shoes. Wearing white in winter? Oh well. Maybe the famous international designer, "Hoar Frost", is simply starting a new trend?

One Head... Many Legs... and Patience

Winter on Eighty Acres finds whitetail deer gathering together for protection and to save energy by using well worn trails through the deep snow. Pictured is a young doe whose head is framed within the herd's legs. So far, the deer herd looks strong and healthy. They will need to wait about seven weeks before the arrival of warmer winds and longer days. Waiting for spring requires patience for the deer as well as me. ▶

Warmed on a Cold Winter Morning

Recently the Earth Mother shivered and sent bitter, gusty northwest winds with temperatures dropping to 22 degrees below zero. The wood stove burned hot and I fed it numerous times during the day with dried oak, elm and birch logs. During the night, the winds calmed and the frosty breath of the Earth Mother quietly crept to my garage windows. With an artist's touch, she spent the entire night drawing elaborate patterns of ice flowers and branches. In the morning, I marveled at the beauty and felt my heart warmed on a cold December morning.

Henry Ford was Wrong

Henry Ford once said, "Chop your own wood and it will warm you twice." By my count I touch each piece of wood six times. Cutting. Splitting. Hauling. Stacking. Feeding the fire. Removing the ashes. Perhaps Henry Ford didn't burn much wood? So... chop your own wood and you are warmed SIX times! A whole lot of work. But I wouldn't change a thing.

Winter Sunset

Bare tree branches and trunks are silhouetted in the evening sky and say farewell to the end of another winter day on Eighty Acres.

Wounded Deer

I first saw the wounded deer in late November. The bowhunter's arrow had severed nerves forcing her to eat only while on her knees. Her remarkable strength and courage allowed her to survive the brutal winter, but by late spring, her strength had ebbed. She finally laid down and went to sleep for the last time near a brushy tree line.

Mindful of a Simple Leaf

Numerous snowfalls, winds, and rains, yet the dried maple leaf hung tightly to its perch. Finally the leaf slipped off and floated downward upon the snow. Like an excited child, I brought my treasure home and gently pressed the leaf between the pages of my old Webster's dictionary. Taped to my living room window, with the morning sunlight in the background, I captured the maple leaf's subtle patterns, textures and beauty. Yes! Mindful of a simple leaf.

Rematch Tomorrow

It is now midwinter on Eighty Acres and the deer are becoming more aggressive and desperate for food. Pictured above are two adult does who are standing on their hind legs doing battle over a few kernels of shelled corn. For a moment they are suspended in air. Like heavyweight boxers, they throw sharp jabs and launch wild punches at each other. Today the victor will claim the scarce food and the loser will need to move on. Tomorrow there will be a rematch.

Snow Shadows

A bright sunny winter day on Eighty Acres and long shadows stretch across the snow white valley. Silent shadows… secret stories… ever moving… soon forgotten.

Woodpecker Tree

Woodpeckers looking for ants, insects and beetle larva used their strong beaks to hammer away on this dead elm tree.

Frozen Sunset

The icicle's fate is sealed. Tomorrow as the sun climbs in the sky, all of her delicate beauty and colors will melt away. But tonight she celebrates her journey by reflecting the beauty of the sunset. Gone tomorrow, but today frozen in my photograph.

A Quiet Goodbye

A full moon over Eighty Acres whispers goodbye to the night and quietly slips away.

Snowbound

At 8:00 a.m., the first snow flakes appeared, swirled and quietly settled on Eighty Acres. For nearly 24 hours it snowed and when the last flake fell, there was a foot of new snow. Snowbound! Nothing to do but feed the fire, curl up in a blanket, read a good book, watch the snow grow high on the porch railing, and simply appreciate the wonder and joy of being snowbound on Eighty Acres. The next day I reluctantly plowed the driveway.

Snowshoe Trails

There are more than two miles of twisting tree lined snowshoe trails on Eighty Acres. Tracks tell me I share the trails with deer, fox, coyotes, turkeys and squirrels. I sometimes bring a thermos of coffee along on my walks. The hot coffee warms my hands, steams my glasses, and for a few moments, stops me on the trails. It is in these quiet moments I listen to the Earth Mother tell me her stories.

Enter if I Dared

After a foot of heavy snow fell on Eighty Acres the woods became dark and foreboding, cautioning me to enter only if I dared.

Thank You Message

Thank you for taking the time to walk with me on Eighty Acres. I sincerely hope you have enjoyed the many photos and stories of the land.

A challenge to me and to you is to be mindful of all the earth has to offer each day. There are many definitions of "mindfulness", but all focus on our efforts to actively process each physical, emotional and mental moment in our lives. If we do so, we will live in the present, experience the voice of the moment and discover that what we once thought ordinary, truly is remarkable.

Enjoy each day! Enjoy each journey!

Bruce Siebold, 2018